The bicycle's great-grandpa was a heavy, clunky thing—

with wooden wheels and wooden spokes,
a wooden saddle, frame, and yoke.

GERMANY
1817

The velocipede, as it was called,
    had no pedals to turn at all.

But gentlemen with muscles and means
    could propel these funny new running machines.

Then off they rolled!

The idea traveled on to America,
    where people bought tickets to examine a replica.

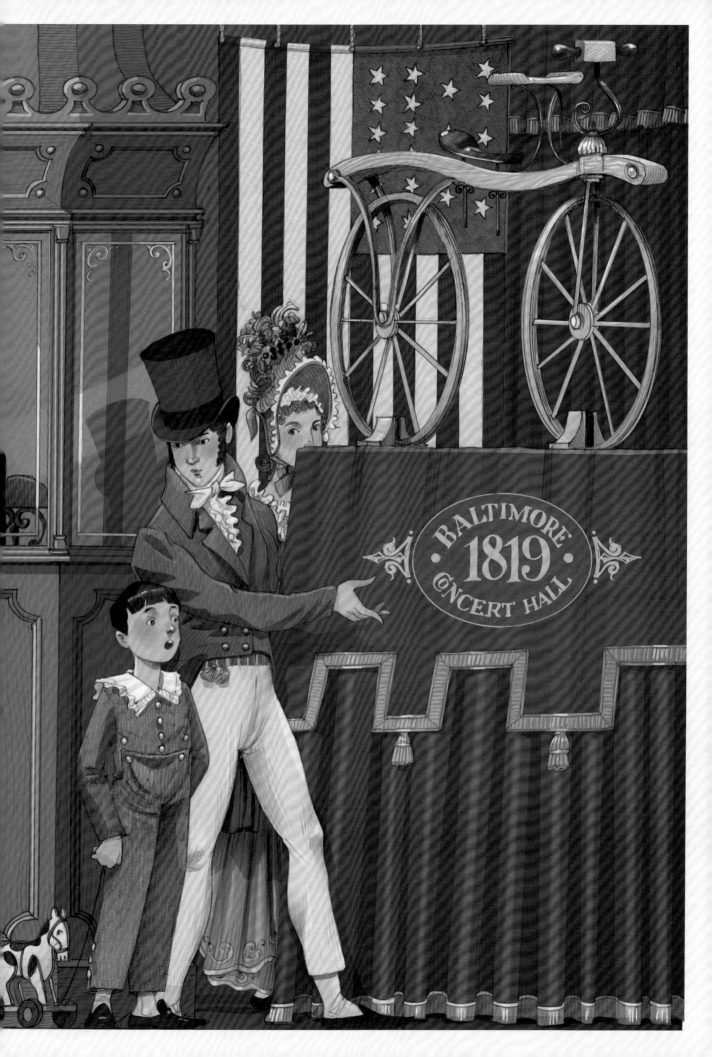

The first velocipedes were thrilling but frightening.
One reporter said they flew "like lightning"!

News of a swift-moving, horse-like creation
careened through big cities and stirred up the nation.

WASHINGTON SQUARE

19

U.S. RIDE

As sidewalks grew rather uncivilized,
angry pedestrians organized.

Laws were written and hastily passed:
No velocipedes on the walking paths!

But American roads were rough and rutty,
dusty, dung-stained, cobbled, muddy.

So velocipedes were left behind
and all but forgotten in one year's time.

While America was wiring up telegraphs
and laying down miles of railroad tracks . . .

wheelers still tinkered with cranks, pulleys, sails, treadles, and levers—ideas that failed.

Then in 1863 . . .

P. LALLEMENT.
VELOCIPEDE.

Patented
No. 59,915

Witnesses

Inventor.
Pierre Lallement

a mechanic in France found a way to revive
the two-wheeled machine with a cool pedal drive.

He sailed with the parts for his solid-iron gadget,
into New York . . . then went on to Connecticut.

1865.

When Pierre Lallement took his very first ride
through the hilly New England countryside,

he ran into a little engineering mistake—
two hundred pounds of accelerating weight . . .

and no brake!

While Lallement struggled to market his notion,
French manufacturers set Paris in motion.

A short while later, in 1868 . . .

a few limber lads with a flying trapeze
balanced on wheels with astonishing ease.

GEORGE

FREDERICK

THE B_ _ SH

1868

In cities like Boston, they raced their new steeds
for loud, cheering crowds who were awed by their speeds.

Suddenly, Americans were talking. Newspapers proclaimed:
VELOCIPEDES COULD BRING AN END TO WALKING!

BOSTON COMMON

AUGUST 1868

But for working-class people, this wasn't reality—
a new set of wheels cost half a year's salary!—

and hard iron tires on harrowing streets
made everyday riding
a bone-shaking feat.

So velocipedes again disappeared,
    but several years later, high-wheelers appeared.

There were towering wheels for sporty high-flyers
    and three-wheeled wonders for less daring riders.

But the bikes of this era were tricky and treacherous
    and still too expensive for all but the prosperous.

1880

SPOON
BRAKES

No. 2[?]005

Fig.2.
SPOKES

f

f

g

g

g

g

g

f

f

PATENTED:
1880

INVENTOR

PENNY FARTHING

ARIEL

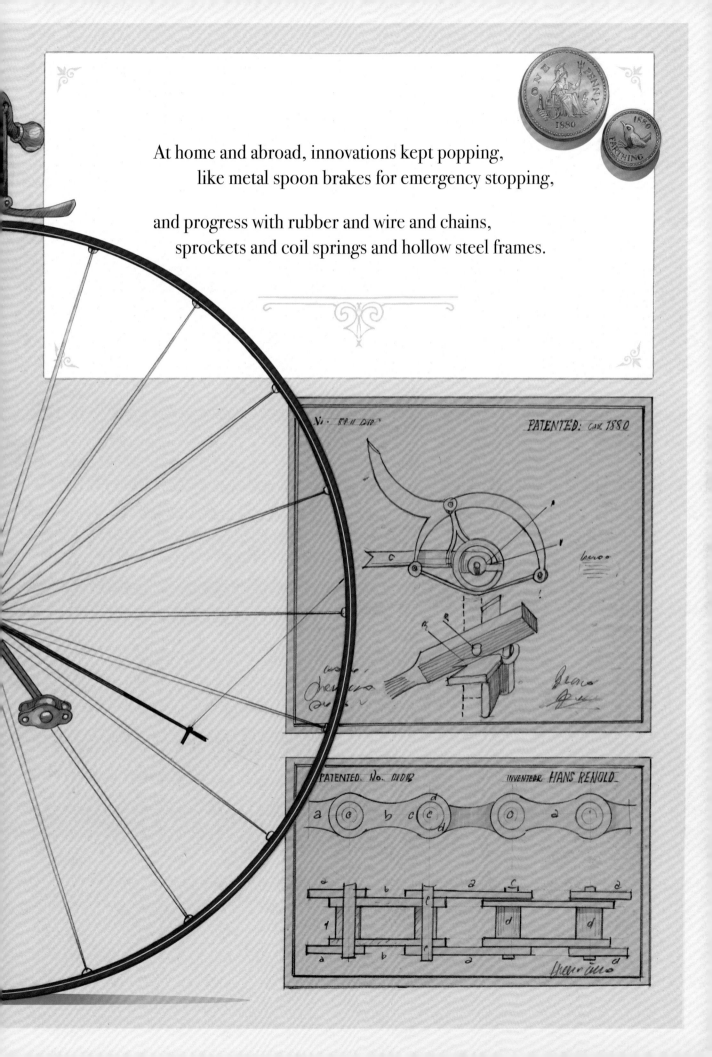

At home and abroad, innovations kept popping,
like metal spoon brakes for emergency stopping,

and progress with rubber and wire and chains,
sprockets and coil springs and hollow steel frames.

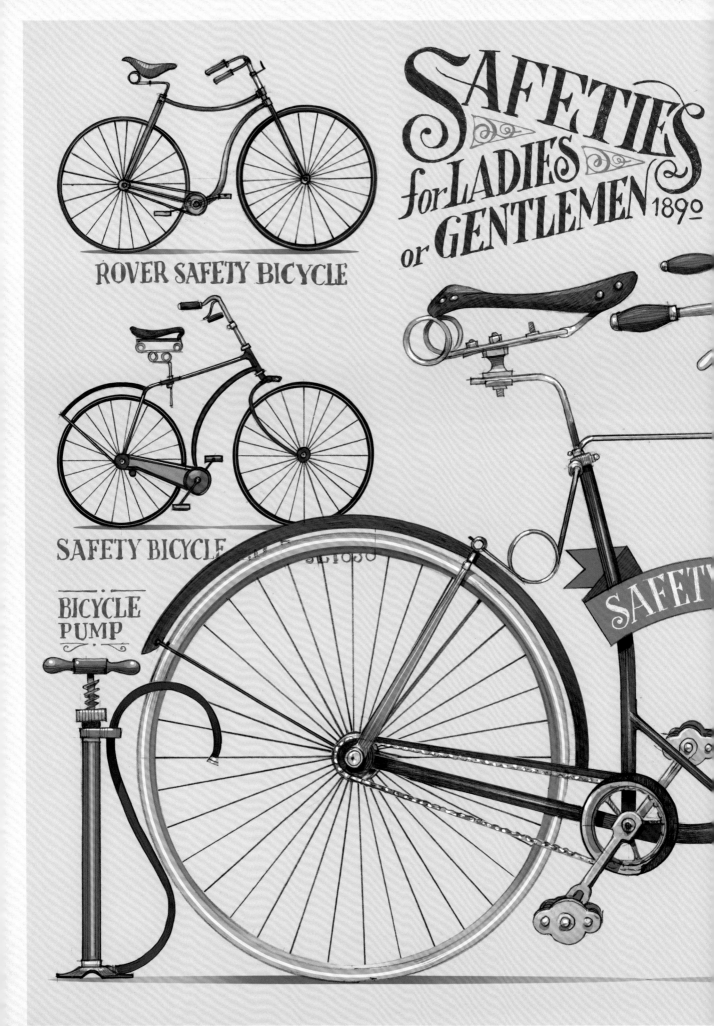

SAFETIES for LADIES or GENTLEMEN 1890

ROVER SAFETY BICYCLE

SAFETY BICYCLE

BICYCLE PUMP

SAFETY

Finally . . .

by the mid-1890s, the bicycles made
    were much like the modern bikes we ride today,

with modest-sized wheels and comfortable seating,
    inflatable tires and slick, easy steering.

They were safer and steadier and lighter and faster.
    Here was a bicycle almost anyone could master.

ONLY $75

PNEUMATIC TIRE

OIL·POWERED
BICYCLE LAMP

Women, especially, were off with a zoom
in split skirts and high boots and bold pantaloons.

Goodbye to petticoats and the waist-clenching corset!
Hello to joy rides on smooth blacktop pavement!

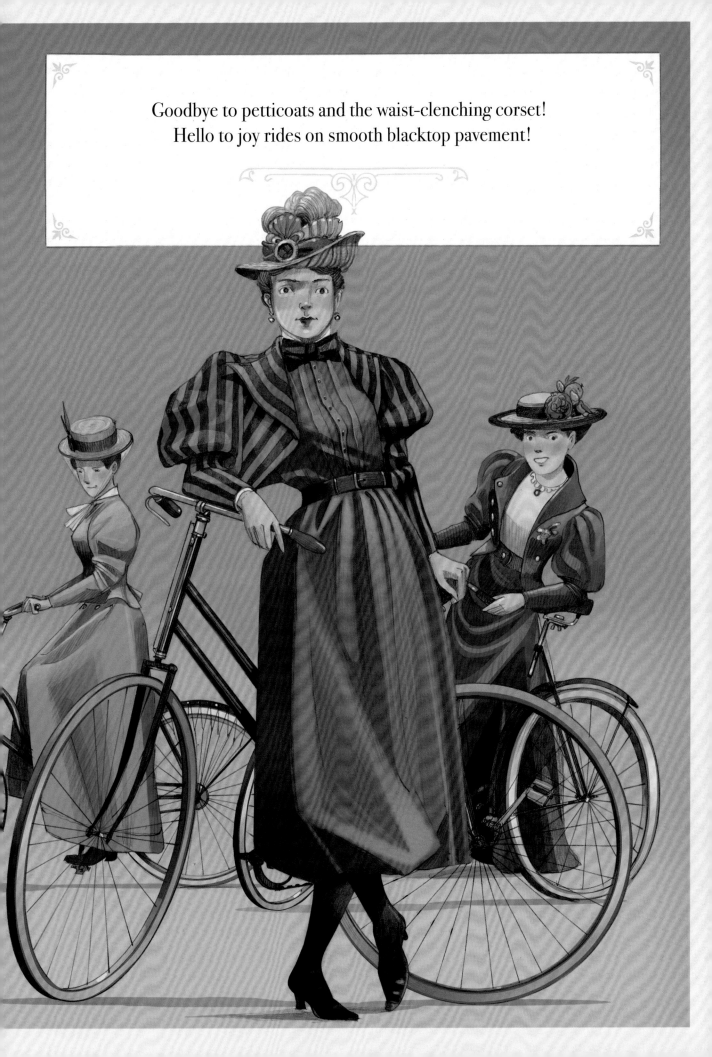

Now two-wheelers sped along streets and parkways
in the 1890s Bicycle Craze.

As the dazzling decade rolled to an end,
bicycle prices began to descend.

Then this radical mechanical horse
became a turn-of-the-century
world-changing force—

no more just a toy for the wealthier classes,
but pedal-powered freedom
for the big, bustling masses.

More About Bicycles

For more than one hundred years before the first bicycle, inventors worked to create human-powered vehicles. These slow, clumsy "horseless carriages" were usually powered by servants who sweated over levers and cranks. Sensible people knew they were better off walking.

In 1817, a German inventor named Karl Drais built the first pedal-less two-wheeler. It had many names, including draisine, running machine, and dandy horse. Drais's idea traveled to various parts of Europe in 1818. The French called it the velocipede—meaning "fast feet"—and this was one of the names that stuck.

That same year, an English coach-maker named Denis Johnson improved upon Drais's design. Using both iron and wood parts, Johnson gave his "hobby horse" a lighter frame, a simpler steering rod, and footrests for coasting. Wealthy young men rolled through London that year, creating both a sensation and a nuisance.

Velocipedes arrived in the United States in 1819. From the start, they were awe-inspiring—most people had never moved so fast unless they were riding a horse. But the rutty and muddy unpaved roads of the early 1800s were almost impassable for two-wheelers. On the sidewalks, velocipedes frequently caused crashes and injuries. Americans rejected the velocipede that same year.

In both Europe and America, inventors returned to making human-powered machines with three and four wheels. Some of the machines became toys for children. Some evolved into the first wheelchairs for people with disabilities. But most of these inventions just never worked very well.

Eventually, a young French mechanic named Pierre Lallement experimented with the original running-machine design. In 1863, he built what many historians believe was the first pedal-powered two-wheeler. It had a solid-iron frame, stiff wooden wheels, and weighed about 70 pounds, but it was a radical breakthrough.

In 1865, Lallement traveled to the United States with parts for a second velocipede. He settled in Connecticut, where he shocked and thrilled the people who saw him ride. Lallement continued to work on his velocipede and patented it in 1866, but he couldn't find a US manufacturer.

Meanwhile, French entrepreneurs, who must have seen Lallement riding his original two-wheeler in Paris, started building a nearly identical cycle. In 1867, Pierre Michaux and his collaborators began selling pedal velocipedes in Paris. Many Parisians adored them. Soon, other French manufacturers were making and selling velocipedes, and cycling spread across Europe and the world.

In 1868, European velocipedes reached America when a touring English acrobat troupe called the Hanlon-Lees featured cycling on stages throughout the United States. To drum up excitement and sell more tickets to their evening shows, the Hanlon-Lees also raced their machines in public. American enthusiasm for velocipedes was immediate. In almost no time, American carriage manufacturers began churning out cycles. Riding rinks, schools, clubs, and races popped up in every city.

However, the 1868–1869 cycling boom was short-lived in America because roads hadn't improved much since 1819. Hard wooden wheels, iron tires, and the overall poor construction of these machines also gave cyclists a very uncomfortable ride. In fact, velocipedes were nicknamed "boneshakers" because riding one was such a bumpy, body-rattling experience.

For the next few years, the bicycle, as it was now called, changed in big ways. High-wheel bicycles were first developed in Europe and later gained popularity in the United States. Their giant front wheel rolled farther than previous wheels with each push of the pedal and absorbed some of the shock from the roads. But getting onto the seat of a high-wheeler was a little like mounting a moving horse, and riders often took tumbles before they could even get rolling. When a cyclist did make it out on the road, the precarious contraption was accident-prone. If the front wheel hit a bump, a rider could be sent flying headfirst over the handlebars.

In 1885, an English bike builder named John Kemp Starley created the Rover Safety Bicycle. With chain drive, these bicycles didn't need tall wheels to roll fast or go far. In the late 1880s, American "safeties" hit the streets. A few years later, the fast, cushy inflatable tire arrived. Suddenly, bicycles were everywhere.

The 1890s Bicycle Craze brought important changes. Women, who were previously confined at home or in factories, began to go places independently— without chaperones and wearing pants. Before bicycles, doctors cautioned against overexertion, but bikes helped prove that vigorous exercise was healthy (even for women). Streets were improved and the first highways were built because cyclists demanded smooth pavement. In time, bicycles became cheap daily transportation for millions of ordinary people.

Today, more than a billion bicycles are in use all over the world—for fun, for exercise, and for going places. In countries such as China, Japan, Denmark, and the Netherlands, bicycling is still one of the most popular and convenient ways to get around. Bicycles also have health and environmental benefits; bikes build muscles and never pollute. The average American could save a gallon of gasoline each day by riding a bicycle instead of driving. Many US cities are trying to make cycling safer and easier by constructing special bike lanes on streets and building more and better off-street trails. Together, we could pedal our way to a happier, healthier world.

SELECTED BIBLIOGRAPHY

Guroff, Margaret. *The Mechanical Horse: How the Bicycle Reshaped American Life*. Austin: University of Texas Press, 2016.

Herlihy, David V. *Bicycle: The History*. New Haven, CT: Yale University Press, 2004.

U.S. Energy Information Administration. "U.S. Household Spending for Gasoline Is Expected to Remain Below $2000 for 2017." October 6, 2017. https://www.eia.gov/todayinenergy/detail.php?id=33232.

For my dad, who taught me how to ride
SN

For Francesca—
to the road we've traveled together so far,
and to the wild rides that still await us
IB

The author and publisher wish to extend special thanks to historian David Herlihy, whose extensive research and writing on bicycle history helped inspire and inform this book and who generously reviewed the manuscript for accuracy.

We would also like to note that the patent numbers shown in illustrations are invented and that some creative interpretation has been allowed in the depictions.

Text copyright © 2024 by Sarah M. Nelson
Illustrations copyright © 2024 by Iacopo Bruno

First edition 2024

Library of Congress Catalog Card Number 2022905678
ISBN 978-1-5362-1392-8

24 25 26 27 28 29 CCP 10 9 8 7 6 5 4 3 2 1

Printed in Shenzhen, Guangdong, China

This book was typeset in Bodoni.
The illustrations were done in pencil and colored digitally.

Candlewick Press
99 Dover Street
Somerville, Massachusetts 02144

www.candlewick.com